Birds
of
North America
Mark Rauzon

Bison Books

First Published in 1987 by
Bison Books Ltd
176 Old Brompton Road
London SW5
England

Copyright © 1987 Bison Books Ltd

All rights reserved. No part of this pub-
lication may be reproduced, stored in a
retrieval system or transmitted in any
form by any means, electronic, mechanical, photocopying or otherwise without first obtaining written permission of
the copyright owner.

ISBN 0 86124 345 5

Page 1: In a rare (for hummingbirds)
still moment, this **Broad-Billed Hummingbird** rests on a branch in its mountain habitat in Southern New Mexico
and Arizona.

Page 2-3: Nicknamed by farmers the
'cherrybird,' **Cedar Waxwings** love
fruit, and often gregariously pass fruit
from one beak to another until the fruit
is swallowed or returned to the original
'picker.' They congregate in the Southern US wherever dried berries are
abundant.

Below and opposite: **The Black Oystercatcher** spends late May in California,
flying within 10 days thereafter to
Alaska. When approached, it utters a
shrill whistle and is sure to be joined in
ear-splitting concert by other Oyster-
catchers in the vicinity.

Designed by Cindy Swanson

Picture Credits:
Orville Andrews: 78
Bill Bass, CAS: 16
©Daniel Lee Brown: 1, 25 (bottom), 26 (upper
left), 35 (top), 43 (top), 52-53, 54-55, 69 (top), 86
©David Campbell: 76 (bottom)
Stephen Cress, CU: 95 (bottom)
©Mike Danzenbaker: 4-5, 43 (bottom), 53
(upper right and lower right), 54 (top and lower
left), 73 (lower left), 84, 88, 89 (top)
Robert Drieslin, USFWS: 11 (lower right)
Bill Dyer, CU: 37 (upper right)
William Grenfell: 2-3, 11 (top), 23, 35 (bottom),
44, 69 (top), 70-71, 72, 75, 89 (lower left), 91
(bottom)
©Douglas Herr: 8, 9 (top), 15 (left and right), 17
(top and bottom), 20 (upper left), 20-21, 28,
30-31, 33, 36-37, 40 (top), 41, 46, 48-49, 49,
50-51, 56, 59 (top and lower right), 61, 62,
(upper left), 62-63, 71 (top)
Lloyd G Ingles: 26-27, 42, 58, 67 (lower right),
68, 69 (bottom), 70 (top),
©Peter La Tourette: 6, 7, 10, 12 (lower left), 13,
14, 18, 19 (top), 20 (lower left), 22, 24, 25 (top),
26 (lower left), 29 (top and bottom), 31 (right),
32, 34, 39 (upper right)
Jim Leupold, USFWS: 37 (lower right)
Wayne Lynch, Parks Canada: 39 (lower right),
50 (upper left), 57, 71 (bottom), 80 (top and
bottom), 82
Tom Meyers: 64

Pat McCloskey, Parks Canada: 76 (top)
Parks Canada: 49 (lower right), 60 (top), 66-67,
83 (top), 87
©Mark Rauzon: 9 (lower right), 12 (top), 19
(lower right), 39 (upper left), 40 (lower left), 47,
60 (bottom), 67 (upper right), 74, 79, 81, 85, 90,
91 (top), 92 (upper and lower left), 92-93, 94, 95
(center), 96
GW Robinson: 65
Tom Smylie, USFWS: 65 (upper right)
US Department of Agriculture: 83 (bottom)
US National Park Service: 45 (top), 62 (bot-
tom), 75 (bottom), 77
Donald White, USFWS: 95 (top)
John Woods: 38
©Bill Yenne: 45 (bottom)

Table of Contents

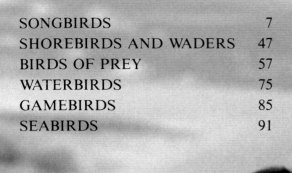

SONGBIRDS

Songbirds, or perching birds, belong to the order of passerines. As a group, they comprise about one-third of all living bird families. Passerines are considered the most advanced bird group since they have evolved from older stock. Several structural characteristics tie this diverse group together. They perch with three toes forward and one backward. As a result, they can effectively cling to narrow branches, wires and reeds without loosing their grip. Their extraordinary ability to vocalize distinguishes these birds from all other animals. It is interesting to note that only in this most advanced order can birds 'talk' by mimicking the human voice. Finally, they are among the most colorful species.

Songbirds communicate with each other through calls and songs. Individuals of many species maintain close contact with call notes, frequently repeated single notes issued by both sexes. Singing is done primarily by males. To advertise nesting and feeding territories, a vast array of chirps, whistles and warbles spill out in liquid phases from the most accomplished songsters like thrushes and orioles. Others, like crows and jays, repeat harsh, broken phases over and over again. But how does one explain a mockingbird singing in the middle of the night; or a fervent chorus greeting a spring morning? It appears that birds also sing just because they feel like making music.

In the spring, males of many species assume their breeding colors, and drab winter hues are exchanged for bright summertime colors. Indeed, what a show! Painted Buntings are a palate of reds, greens, blues. Scarlet Tanagers glow with an intensity of color. Violet-green Swallows shimmer with iridescence. Even among the less colorful species, beautiful arrangements of brown hues or striking displays of black and white astound and confound the eye.

Colors, like songs, serve as individual advertisement. On the breeding grounds, the ardor runs high. In order to mate, a male must beat the competition by excelling in the full repertoire of displays and songs. Tail spots, crests, wingbars and songs are all incorporated into the breeding display. Females maintain a low profile since they generally assume the incubation duties. With dull plumage and quiet calls, their presence is kept a secret from predators. At the end of the mating season, the males too grow silent. Both sexes concentrate on feeding the fast-growing chicks. Eating the summer's bounty, the birds put on layers of fat to fuel their energy needs.

As the seasons change, so do bird plumages. Males' splendor fades to blend with the environment. Many species of songbirds assume a uniform green plumage. Those males that were so distinctive in spring join the females and now appear virtually identical. Traveling in flocks of mixed species or alone, most passerines migrate south at night to avoid detection by predators. Scientists are still studying the details of bird migration, but it appears that birds orient to the celestial

constellations and magnetic polarities of the earth. Birds also take advantage of the local weather conditions. Large flocks have been detected by radar flying south with advancing cold fronts. Most of the insect-eating birds fly to the forests of Central and South America. Bobolinks migrate from the Canadian prairies to the Argentine pampas—a journey of over 3000 miles each way. Some northern species like Wheatears and Arctic Warblers cross the oceans to winter in Asia or Africa.

continued on page 9

The Hooded Oriole *(above)* ranges from southwestern New Mexico to southern California, and its harsh call fills the dense thickets of lowlands that it loves. It lays three to five brown-spotted bluish white eggs. Nesting as high as the tree line in the western US and Canada, the **White-crowned Sparrow** *(opposite)* could, due to its black-and-white facial markings, be mistaken for a chickadee. They eat berries, seeds and insects.

In spring the migration process is reversed. As the days lengthen, birds begin to molt into breeding plumage. Unlike the somber fall migration, spring migration is a well-publicized event. Many species are in full song and breeding dress. The birds continue to fly by night with advancing warm fronts or low systems. As the forests break into bud and flower, a new generation of insects emerge. On their way back to their northern territories, hungry songbirds glean swarming insects from trees and bushes. Without this annual pulse of birds, insects would cause immense damage to crops and forests. However, the vagaries of spring weather can deal a deathly blow to early birds. Late winter snows freeze birds already weakened from extensive flying. Generally, songbirds live only a few years.

Eastern Kingbirds *(left)* are commonly observed harassing crows and birds of prey. This behavior, known as mobbing, also occurs in other passerine families.

Larks and **pipits** are two families of birds that share windswept plains, alpine meadows and seashores. They nest and feed on the ground and their cryptic brown plumage camouflages them well from avian predators. Rather than hop, as most birds do, these terrestrial species walk searching for insects and seeds. Only the **Horned Lark** *(above and right)* species occurs in North America, and it is marked by a fleshy projectile above each eye. It breeds in meadows and winters in large flocks in fields.

Swallows are familiar backyard birds. Many people have marveled at their erratic flight at breakneck speeds as they pick insects out of the air. Swallows are highly migratory. They arrive just after the first insect broods are hatching, and depart for warmer climes when the aerial insect population drops. The reddish-colored swallow species have greatly benefited from their association with man for they nest under eaves and bridges across America. It is hard to imagine where **Barn Swallows** *(above)* nested before farmers came to America.

Perhaps the most famous swallows are of Capistrano, California. Known as **Cliff Swallows** *(left and lower right)* elsewhere, these birds plaster adobe nests on the sheltered sides of buildings and bridges. They repeatedly fly to a local mud source where they collect the mud in their broad bills. Like master masons, they build an inverted nest mouthful by mouthful, and in so doing seem to defy gravity. **Cave Swallows** also breed in loose colonies of mud nests. The behavior of these birds gave rise to the myth that they burrow into the mud each winter and re-emerge the following spring.

Shrikes are medium-sized, masked birds that hunt insects, small mammals, reptiles and birds. With strong feet for holding prey and a hooked bill for tearing, shrikes hunt from exposed perches in open country. When prey is spotted, the shrike swoops in low over the ground and strikes. The prey is taken to a favorite perch and is often impaled on thorns or barbed wire. Shrikes sometimes store prey in this manner, thereby meriting the moniker 'butcher birds.' The Northern Shrike breeds in the Arctic. In winter the species moves into southern Canada and the northern US. This area is the breeding ground of the **Loggerhead Shrike,** *(left)* which, in turn, winters in the southern states.

Waxwings sing thin, trilling notes from atop fruiting trees. Flocks boldly descend on ornamental shrubs around houses and parks to gorge on berries, sometimes becoming intoxicated on fermented fruit. They are crested birds with masked faces and attractive fawn-colored plumage. Waxwings derive their common name from red droplets on the tips of their wings. Like the shrikes, two species of waxwings share a summer and winter range. The **Bohemian Waxwing** *(above)* of the north moves into the summer range of the **Cedar Waxwing** *(right)* in the winter.

House and Bewick Wrens are found around abandoned farms and weedy lots. **Marsh Wrens** *(above left and right),* as well as Sedge and Carolina wrens inhabit moist fields and swamps where rank vegetation provides dense cover. Rock and Canyon Wrens hunt spiders, insects and other small invertebrates in the rocky areas of the West. The largest and most distinctive wren, the **Cactus Wren,** nests amid a fortress of spines in the desert. It sits atop a needled perch and sings throughout the scorching desert day *(left).*

Dippers, or Water Ousels, *(below)* look like plump giant wrens with short stubby tails. However, they act like no other wren would dare. Indeed, few other birds plunge into frigid mountain streams to feed. With the help of their wings, Dippers walk along the stream bottom and seize insects from under rocks and logs. On dry land they constantly bob as if to keep warm.

Actually, they are insulated by waterproof feathers. **Thrashers** *(left)* sing a variety of songs, with each species adding a unique twist to the tune. Songs are sung from conspicuous perches to proclaim the bird on its territory. In the arid West, the **Curve-billed Thrasher** *(above)* uses its stout beak and strong legs to dig in the leaf litter for insects, spiders and scorpions.

The bluebird is another familiar thrush. In recent years, the Eastern Bluebird has been recovering its population numbers. Like Purple Martins, bluebirds must contend with aggressive starlings displacing them from suitable nesting sites. However, as a result of recent conservation efforts, they are returning to nest boxes built specifically to exclude starlings. The **Western Bluebird** *(left)* is still common in oak groves and abandoned fields. Both bluebirds share the robins' red breast, but are blue on the wings and black. Mountain Bluebirds are solid blue and appear to reflect the 'big sky' country they inhabit.

Thrushes are among the finest singers. Their flutelike songs, sung from the deep forest shade, embody the magic of nature. But one need not venture far from home to enjoy a thrush serenade. Each evening in suburbs across America, the robin chorus can be heard. Nesting in shrubs and fruit trees, the **Robin** *(above)* is one of the most familiar birds in America. More people have learned the fundamentals of ornithology from robins than from any other species. Children of all ages have peered into 'robin red breast' nests to find blue egg shells or downy chicks. Not all robins are red breasted. Albinism *(lower right),* or the lack of normal pigmentation, occurs infrequently.

Chickadees are acrobats at the bird feeder in winter; they hang upside down or flit about nervously to investigate a new food source or anyone imitating their whistled calls. All members of this family are similar in coloration but vary where black marks accent. Each species has a dark cap and bib and a light belly. Only the **Chestnut-backed Chickadee** *(right)* of the Pacific coast has a rich brown back, and the **Mountain Chickadee** *(above)* and the Bridled Titmouse are masked. Titmice differ from chickadees by sporting a crest. Chickadees and titmice nest in old woodpecker nests or tree boles. During seasons when there is ample food, several broods may be raised. In the winter, chickadees and titmice join other species in feeding flocks. They are ever on the alert for Sharp-shinned Hawks and stay in constant contact with each other with whistled notes.

The elusive **Hermit Thrush** *(below)* is also known as 'the American nightingale.'

Nuthatches appear to be a cross between chickadees and woodpeckers and are so named for their ability to crack acorns and pine cones. Strictly arboreal, they usually reside high in the tree canopy. Four species are found in North American forests. The Red-breasted Nuthatch prefers the cool conifer forests. It discloses itself usually by toy horn sounds and can often be seen climbing head first down a tree trunk, searching every crack and cranny for insects. The **Pygmy Nuthatch** *(above)* is found in the dry pines of the West. Its eastern counterpart is the Brown-headed Nuthatch of the coastal pines. The **White-breasted Nuthatch** *(left)* is found both in deciduous trees and conifers.

The largest family of songbirds in North America is made up of sparrows, buntings, grosbeaks and finches. All have a conical-shaped bill adapted to cracking seeds. Sparrows are ground birds colored in variable browns, whites and grays. Although frustrated birders call them 'LBJs,' or little brown jobs, sparrow plumage can be very striking. Sparrow names highlight distinctive field marks: **White-crowned, Golden-crowned, Rufous-crowned** *(above)* **White-throated, Black-throated, Black-chinned, Sharp-tailed, Rufous-winged and Clay-colored.** The gaily marked **Lark Sparrow** stands out as the most beautiful.

Residing in many different habitats across North America, the **Song Sparrow** *(left)* is the most adaptive and widespread species. Generally, it prefers bushy areas where it can forage for seeds and insects and sing its melodic song from a conspicuous perch. Throughout its range, Song Sparrows show variations according to local environments. The Atlantic race is pale in comparison to the giant dark Aleutian race. Placed side by side, they look like different species. Other variable species are the Savannah, Fox and Seaside sparrows and **Juncos** *(right)*. Recently, four junco species were reclassified into one so-called the Dark-eyed Junco. All forms have pink bills and white-edged tail feathers.

Cardinals and grosbeaks are brightly colored songbirds with stout beaks to crack tough seeds pry into and pine cones. **Cardinals** *(above and right)* are conspicuous, backyard birds of eastern North America. Seven states have chosen them as their state bird. During this century, cardinals have expanded their northern and southwestern range. In the Southwest, their range overlaps with the similar Pyrrhuloxia, which inhabits thorny brushlands, and resembles slimmer versions of female cardinals. The Rose-breasted and Black-headed Grosbeaks are medium-sized birds of deciduous forests. They are colorful but inconspicuous as they sing from inside the forest canopy.

Towhees are twice the size of average sparrows. The **Rufous-sided Towhee** *(below)* emerges from the undergrowth calling *drink-your-tea*. The Brown Towhee is common in western suburbs and the Green-tailed Towhee is common in western mountains. Abert's Towhee ranges into the California and Nevada deserts.

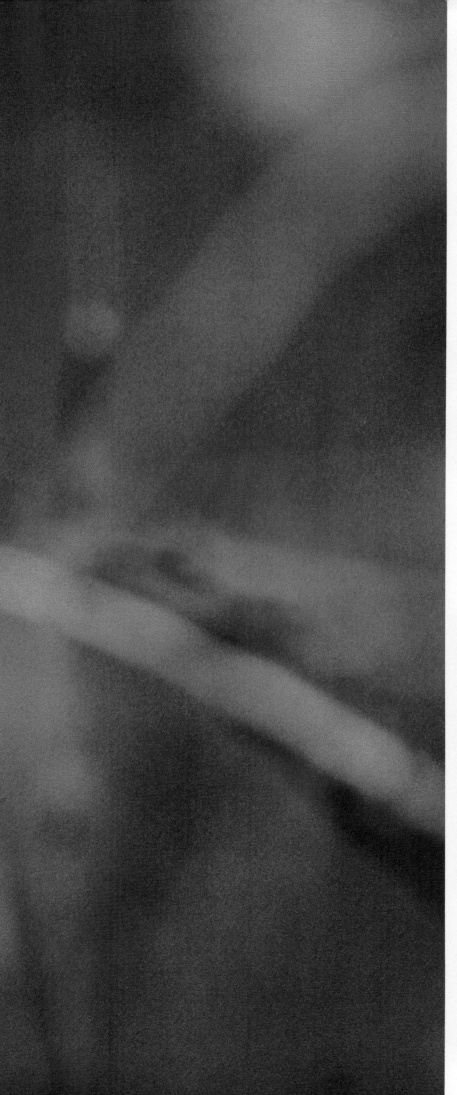

Blue Grosbeaks, **Indigo Buntings** *(left)* and **Lazuli Buntings** *(above),* as their names suggest, are strikingly blue. But perhaps the most colorful of all songbirds is the Painted Bunting. Red underparts, a greenish back and a blue head distinguish this gaudy species from all others. A beautiful bird in white and black is the **Snow Bunting** *(below).* In appearance it is a reverse of the Lark Bunting; it has a white body instead of black and black wing patches in place of white.

Finches are another seed-eating family with variable plumages. American **Goldfinches** *(above)* are mustard yellow during breeding season, turning drab green in the late summer. They fly with characteristic undulations and twittering calls from weedy fields and woodlots. The **Painted Bunting** *(left)* retains its bright colors even in its winter plumage. Like the warblers, its song can be heard around thickets and weedy places along the borders of towns and settlements. Finches are most common in the north, Redpolls breed in spruce and alder forests, and Cassin's Finches fly high in mountain conifer forests. Finches and Buntings belong to the family Fringilidae, which is composed of birds having short, stout beaks adapted for cracking seeds, which family also includes Canaries and Cardinals. Crossbills use their scissorlike beaks to excavate seeds from tough cones.

Wood Warblers *(left)* are the butterflies of the bird world. During spring migration, these gaily feathered bundles of energy flit among the tree tops. Their high-pitched buzzy songs fill the woods as they pick insects from the foliage. Bedecked primarily in yellows, blacks and white, they also show splashes of brilliant color. The **Blackburnian Warbler** *(above)* sports a fire-orange throat. Even the less colorful are a joy to behold, like the strikingly patterned **Black-and-White** and **Blackpoll Warblers.** But only during the breeding season are warblers so colorful. Come fall, they all look alike and can be confused with the less vivacious vireos. **Vireos** are a family of rather drab and sluggish (by warbler standards) insect eaters.

Tanagers are richly colored thrush-sized forest dwellers. With black wings and tail set off by a vibrant red body, the **Scarlet Tanager** *(left)* is one of the most distinctive birds. However, it is rivaled by the **Western Tanager** *(below),* which also has black wings and tail but sports a red head and lemon-yellow body. The South has the brick-red **Summer Tanager** *(above)* and the **Hepatic Tanager.** All are highly migratory insect and fruit eaters.

Orioles are related to blackbirds and share the sharply pointed bill and black highlights. Hoods, masks and wings of black contrast with orange and yellow plumage. The **Northern Oriole** is the most common across the continent in the summer. Formerly known as the **Baltimore Oriole** *(above)* in the East, this species was recently grouped with the **Bullock's Oriole** *(left)* of the West because the two species interbreed where their ranges meet.

The **Bronzed Cowbird** *(below)* deserves special mention due to its peculiar breeding habits. The female lays a series of single eggs in the nests of other songbirds. When each chick hatches, it evicts the other eggs and chicks from the nest. The foster parent assumes the responsibility of caring for the quickly growing chick. As a result, the parasitic cowbird causes small species like vireos and buntings to become increasingly rare. The cowbird is inadvertently assisted by farmers who remove woodlots to expand agricultural lands that, in turn, provide food for the cowbirds.

Aggressive and bold, intelligent and curious—these are family characteristics of jays, crows and magpies. Their raucous cries and conspicuous presence make them familiar to everyone. The **Blue Jay** of the deciduous forest is common in backyards yet very secretive when breeding. In the West, the **Steller's Jay** *(left)* is common in coniferous forests and the **Scrub Jay** *(above right)* inhabits suburban yards and chaparral. They frequent campsites to beg and steal food from unwary campers. In the northern fir forests, the Gray Jay flys like a ghost. Beware, this quiet jay is also a camp robber! The western mountains are home to **Clark's Nutcracker.** Named by the Lewis and Clark expedition, this jay-like bird pries seeds out of pinecones with its long bill. The brown, green and gray-breasted jays are tropical species and barely enter the southwestern region.

Two species of magpies are found in North America, both having long sweeping tails and black and white plumage. Black-billed Magpies are winter scavengers that fight coyotes and ravens over dead carcasses. In the summer, pairs nest in massive stick nests. **Yellow-billed Magpies** *(above)* are slightly smaller than the black-billed species and are unique to California's agricultural valleys.

Several species of American crows are virtually identical. The lustrous black, **Common** *(right)* and **Northwestern Crows** are distinguishable only by their voices. They inhabit a variety of environments, and can be found scavenging near human settlements or along the shoreline

The **Raven** is the largest songbird but it can only muster croaks. Usually seen in pairs coursing over mountainous terrain, the raven commands a certain dignity lacking in smaller crows. Because it winters in the Arctic, it is no wonder that Indian and Eskimo legends convey godlike wisdom to this jet-black bird in the snow-white landscape.

Woodpeckers

Woodpeckers do not belong in the songbird order since they have only two forward toes, but they are included here because they have similar habits. With two front toes and two rear toes for grasping bark and a supporting set of tail feathers to lean on, woodpeckers can securely drill into dead or living wood. By rapping on the wood and listening to the sound, woodpeckers can locate burrowing beetle larvae and termite colonies. The task of pecking wood then begins in earnest. Using their sharp, chisel-like bill and protected by a shock-absorbing skull, woodpeckers excavate their prey and build new nest holes each year. Previous nest holes are eagerly sought by owls, flycatchers, chickadees and many other birds.

North American woodpeckers have ranged from the raven-sized and now probably extinct Ivory-billed Woodpecker to sparrow-sized **Downy Woodpecker. Acorn Woodpeckers** *(above)* are medium-sized colonial nesters. They cache acorns in telephone poles and old dead branches *(left)* for common use. The **Red-Cockaded Woodpecker** uses its environment to advantage. After pecking through the bark, it assists pine resin to form a sticky defense against climbing snakes. Sapsuckers, such as the **Red-breasted Sapsucker** *(right)* and the **Yellow-bellied Sapsuckers** drill rows of small holes in certain trees. The flowing sap attracts insects, which the sapsucker laps up with its brush-tipped tongue.

Hummingbirds

If warblers are the butterflies then hummingbirds are the bumblebees of the bird world. Indeed, the **Calliope Hummingbird** *(overleaf, lower right),* the smallest bird in North America, is barely larger than a big bee. 'Hummers' build a nest of spider webs and lichen to lay pea-sized eggs. They evoke a spirit of unbounded energy, which is a direct result of high-calorie foods. Sipping flower nectar fuels their ultra-fast flight—up to 80 wing beats per second! Only the **Ruby-throated** species occurs regularly in the East. The West hosts the **Rufous** *(left and overleaf, upper right),* **Costa's** *(overleaf, at left)* and **Anna's** *(above and below)* hummingbirds.

SHOREBIRDS AND WADERS

Life is abundant at the water's edge, and a wide diversity of birds thrive in this nutrient-rich environment. Shorebirds and waders frequent the zone where nutrients from the land mix with fresh and salt waters. Ranging in height from 5 inches to 5 feet, shorebirds and waders utilize many different hunting techniques throughout a wide range of environments. Picking, probing, sifting or stabbing, these birds secure their food in all depths of shallow water. Waders like cranes, herons and egrets patiently stalk their prey. An instant stab with their lethal bills and unwary prey are secured. Shorebirds randomly probe the mud with their sensitive bills to locate worms and invertebrates. Plovers seize insects from open plains and mudflats. Upturned bills of avocets sweep small organisms from the shallows. Phalaropes, the only swimming shorebirds, stir up food with their partially webbed feet.

Waders such as egrets, herons and ibises nest together in colonies secure from predators. Bitterns and rails conceal their nests in dense marsh vegetation. Cranes build their nests on the ground in marsh and tundra areas, but must be ready to defend against predators at any moment. Shorebirds, on the other hand, rely on cryptic coloration to camouflage eggs and chicks. Chicks are mobile when hatched and capable of running and hiding expertly. Many species of shorebirds nest in the Arctic, and must raise their broods during the brief summers. The young grow quickly and prepare to leave the breeding grounds by early August. Shorebirds are strong, swift fliers capable of long migrations over water. Many winter on the shores of South America. Waders also migrate to warmer climates, going as far as Central and South America. Waders like ibises and spoonbills fly in V-shaped lines similar to geese while shorebirds fly in dense flocks perfectly coordinated for evasive maneuvers.

Great Blue Herons *(left)* stalk fish, amphibians, reptiles and small mammals in marshes and lakes across North America. Their 6-foot wingspan, retracted neck and slow, deliberate wing beats characterize this bird in flight. Herons build flimsy stick nests in trees near water. The Tricolored Heron and Reddish Egret dance with wings outstretched to scare fish from hiding. A solitary marsh bird, the Little Blue Heron stands slightly over 2 feet tall and has a sinuous neck and daggerlike bill. The one-foot-tall Green Heron is the smallest of the group. A tall, majestic heron is the **American Egret** *(below)*.

American Bitterns *(left)* are well-camouflaged denizens of dense reedy marshes. Colored in mute browns and blacks, they blend in superbly with their world. When confronted with a predator, they freeze with their bill pointing skyward and seem to disappear.

Roseate Spoonbills *(above)* stand out as the most beautiful yet bizarre bird of North America. With naked green heads, pink bodies and ornamental feather tufts, spoonbills look like something from *Alice in Wonderland*. They sweep their unique bills through saltwater marshes to capture fish.

Cranes and their smaller relatives, the rails, gallinules, and coots, breed in marshes throughout North America. The grandest member is the Whooping Crane. Standing nearly six feet tall, this species has been brought back from the edge of extinction. With help from **Sandhill Cranes** *(above),* the population has climbed from a precipitous 20 birds to almost 100. Wildlife biologists placed Whooping Crane eggs under foster Sandhill Cranes, and the Sandhills raised the young like their own. The young Whoopers followed the Sandhills during migration and cut hundreds of dangerous miles from their traditional migration route.

Clapper Rails *(right)* are voices of the marsh. The typical rail is seldom seen but often heard. The Black Rail is the smallest family member. Barely 4 inches high, these birds prefer running instead of flying. They look like scurrying mice but can not fool **Black-crowned Night Herons** *(below),* who eat rails when high tides flood the marshes.

Along rocky coastlines, American Oystercatchers and **Black Oyster-catchers** *(left)* are never quiet for long. The Black Oystercatcher pipes out a warning *kleep-kleep-kleep.* Its red, chisel-like bill is laterally compress-ed. With a quick jab, it pries open shellfish to each the protein-rich meat.

Seemingly forever in motion, the diminutive Sanderling runs after retreat-ing waves. It must quickly hunt before the next wave crashes. The **Marbled Godwit** *(below)* wades knee deep in seafoam. Its recurved bill probes for marine worms, clams and crabs. The **Willet** *(above)* hides its boldly pat-terned wings until it explodes into flight. The sudden display alarms would-be predators.

At margins of quiet bays and estuaries, many species of shorebirds feed in different manners. **Whimbrels** use their decurved bills to catch small clams in deeper water. In the shallows. **Black-necked Stilts** *(below)* pick at the surface. **Short** and **Long-billed dowitchers** frantically needle the mud with their 5-inch beaks. With their upturned bills, **Avocets** *(above)* filter organisms from the soupy mud.

Short-legged sandpipers, collectively known as 'peeps,' run along the beach to seize sandfleas and flies. **Least, Weater,** and **Semipalmated Sand-pipers** are nearly identical and vary by only millimeters in bill length. The unmistakable **Long-billed Curlew** *(right)* probes crab burrows with its 9-inch bill or chases grasshoppers in prairies where it breeds.

BIRDS OF PREY

Birds of prey are the largest and most powerful birds. Their visual acuity, hearing and strength are exceptional. Eating live or dead insects, fish, reptiles, amphibians, birds and mammals places them at the top of the food chain. Generally, the group can be divided into day-hunting hawks, vultures, and falcons and night-hunting owls. Wing shape indicates a great deal about what the bird of prey eats and how it hunts. Broad wings are used for soaring and quick maneuvering. Soaring birds spot prey from above while other broad-winged birds give chase. Narrow, pointed wings are designed for speed, and birds strike in the air or hover and pounce.

America's symbol of freedom is a striking bird built for power. A massive yellow beak, white head and tail and dark brown body mark the adult **Bald Eagle** *(below)*. Bald Eagles are fisheaters and are found around lakes, rivers and seacoasts. Alaska supports the largest population. Elsewhere, they are classified as a threatened or endangered species. Eagles mate for life and return to the same nest sites, usually in tall trees each spring. The pair renew their bond with spectacular mating flights, diving at each other, locking talons and tumbling in flight. Usually two young are raised each year. Juveniles remain mottled brown until their fourth year, when they molt into adult plumage. Eagles steal food and scavenge dead fish. It was this behavior that led Benjamin Franklin to suggest they they were perhaps inappropriate symbols for a new nation, as might also be the case with the **Goshawk** *(opposite),* a fierce and sometimes destructive hunger.

Golden Eagles *(left),* are the most powerful birds of North America. Although they can kill prey five times their own weight, they eat mainly rabbits and ground squirrels. They even eat carrion when live prey is scarce. Eagles are completely protected by law but are still occasionally shot by sheep ranchers who claim that the birds kill lambs. Golden Eagle nests are called aeries, stick nests built on high cliff ledges. Here, eagles nest for generations. Eagle territories must be over 30 square miles to provide enough food to support breeding efforts. Young eagles learn to fly on strong mountain winds and become masterful fliers.

Kites are long-winged tropical hawks, four species of which occur in North America. With a white head and belly and black flight feathers, the **Swallow-tailed Kite***(above)* is the most beautiful bird of prey. This graceful bird manifests a long V-shaped tail and narrow wings. In the forests of the Southeast, these birds nest semicolonially in tall trees and hunt snakes, amphibians and flying insects.

The **Snail** or **Everglade Kite** hunts apple snails, its sole food, in the grasslands of the Florida Everglades. It extracts the snail meat with its specialized hooked beak. Loss of wetland habitat due to development, drought and fires has placed the Snail Kite in danger of extinction in North America. The Mississippi and the **Black-shouldered Kites** *(right),* have piercing red eyes and gray, black and white plumage. **Black-shouldered Kites** have become increasingly common since they adapted to hunting rodents along highways. Primarily a southern species, they are expanding their range north.

Falcons are narrow-winged hawks of open country. All falcons have pointed wings designed for speed. The smallest falcon, the **Kestrel** *(above and below),* is the most colorful with orange-brown and slate-gray plumage. Kestrels are commonly seen hovering over a spot in a field or sitting on wires intently watching the ground for any signs of movement. They eat insects, mice and small birds.

Merlins *(right)* are a bit larger than Kestrels and eat birds taken on the wing.

Unmatched for speed and skill, **Peregrine Falcons** *(below, as chicks)* can reach speeds of almost 200 miles per hour during hunting dives, killing duck-sized birds upon impact in flight. Pesticides have reduced Peregrine Falcon numbers, but in recent years, they are recovering and returning to nest on skyscrapers and bridges in the East. Peregrines in the West nest on high mountains or sea islands. **Prairie Falcons** *(right)* are similar to the Peregrines. They breed on cliffs in the West and hunt quail and ground squirrels from their rocky perches. The **Arctic Gyrfalcon** *(above)* was once reserved by kings and popes for hunting purposes. Today, Gyrfalcons bring fabulous sums because they are strictly protected and are illegal to possess without permits. They hunt snowshoe hares and large birds for food. During winter food shortages, Gyrfalcons migrate into temperate North America.

Buteos are stocky, broad-winged hawks capable of sustained soaring. They often fly in circles, riding updrafts of warm air. **Red-tailed Hawks** *(above)* are the most common. A very adaptive species, they are found in farmlands, marshes, mountains and deserts across America. Red-tails eat rodents that they can spot while soaring up to one-half mile away. Their piercing scream is frequently imitated by jays. The smaller Red-shouldered Hawks and Broad-winged Hawks are found in forests, where they eat a high percentage of reptiles sighted from perches on tree limbs *(left)*.

Marked with a white rump and black band, the **Rough-legged Hawk** *(below)* is an eagle-like buteo of the North with a wingspan approaching five feet. The Rough-legged Hawk nests on cliffs and hunts rabbits in the artic tundra to feed its chicks *(above)*. This mother **Sharp-shinned Hawk** *(left)* is intent on protecting her young from the intruding photographer. These hawks are common to eastern woodlands and this particular bird was photographed at St Lawrence Island National Park in Canada.

Owls

Owls tend to come to life after hawks, falcons and vultures roost for the night. Like hawks, owls kill with their strong, taloned feet and tear food with their hooked beaks. By means of acute hearing and sight, owls can locate live prey in almost total darkness. Their night vision is over 30 times greater than human vision. Not all owls are night hunters. Some owls hunt by day, proving that owls can also see quite well in bright light. To avoid alerting their prey by feather rustling, owl feathers are feltlike to muffle sounds. Owls lay from 2 to 8 round white eggs.

Long-eared, **Great Horned Owls** *(left)* and **Screech Owls** *(above)* have conspicuous tufts of head feathers that resemble ears but help make the owl look like a branch stump. Great Horned owls are fearless and strong. Hunting by night, they kill raccoons, skunks, rabbits and *(right)* Kangaroo rats.

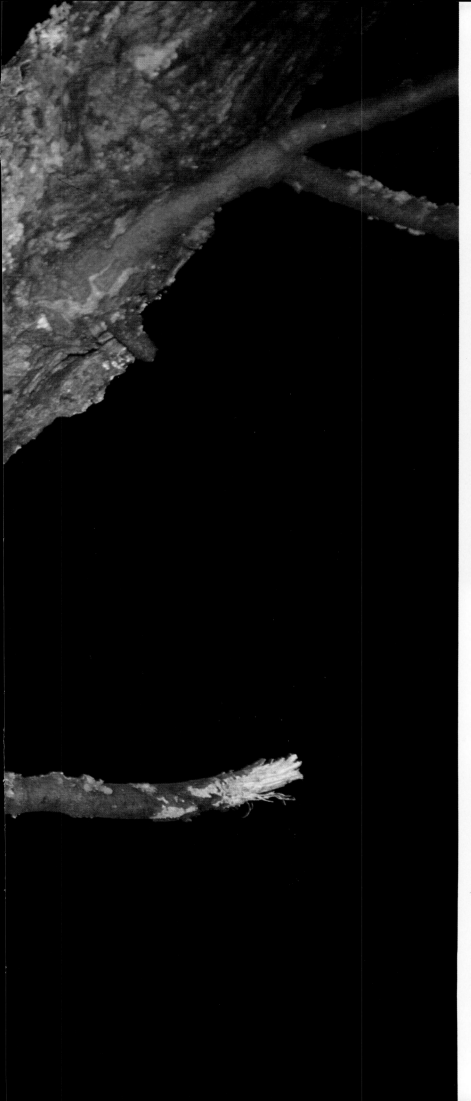

Barn Owls *(above)* have distinctive heart-faced heads and lovely cinnamon-specked white plumage. They live up to their names by frequently nesting in barns and abandoned buildings. Nest sites can be located by finding owl pellets, which are bundles of regurgitated fur and bone. Farmers are happy for their help in keeping the mice population in check. Other large 'earless' owls are the Great Gray and **Snowy Owls** *(above)* that hunt mice and lemmings in the Arctic and Subarctic. During periods of low rodent numbers, they venture into temperate areas in search of food. The **Burrowing Owl** *(below)* stands atop its home, usually an abandoned ground-squirrel burrow, looking for beetles to eat.

The **Short-eared Owl** *(left)* patrols fields in the late afternoons for mice and birds. The call of the **Saw-whet Owl** *(below)* sounds like a saw being sharpened, while the Screech Owl screams. Other owls hoot, bark, shriek, whistle and boom. The Barrel Owl hoots *who cooks for you?* **Hawk Owls** *(above)* are day-flying hunters of northern forests and Barn Owls hunt strictly by night

WATERBIRDS

Migrating high overhead on their southward journey, skeins of geese foretell the coming of winter. From tundra pools of the Arctic, northern lakes and sloughs, from pothole ponds of the upper Midwest, waterbirds of all shapes and sizes repeat the phenomenon of migration. A tradition as ancient as the land itself, birds funnel through four aerial corridors: the Atlantic, Central, Mississippi and Pacific flyways. Along the way, they seek food and protection in marshlands and fields before continuing their journey south.

Biologists have determined migration routes by collecting the metal or plastic bands placed on nestlings. For example, the bands attached to geese on the Arctic breeding grounds have been recovered as far away as South America and Hawaii. Young birds, inexperienced with migration, follow adults to reach the ancestoral wintering grounds, but sometimes they overshoot or make a wrong turn. Strays end up lost at sea or stranded on islands, and in rare cases they colonize new environments. This may be how the Nene, or Hawaiian Goose, evolved from Canada Goose stock lost in Hawaii eons ago.

Waterbirds feed in two basic ways: dabbling and diving. Dabblers feed on seeds and vegetation by submerging their heads below water. In this 'bottoms up' position, they can only reach within a neck's length. They are agile on land and can spring from the water's surface to take flight. Large dabblers like swans are too heavy for this maneuver and must make a running start. Divers have larger feet and smaller wings than the dabblers. They feed by swimming to the pond or ocean floor and rooting for aquatic vegetation and mollusks or by catching fish. To get airborne, they must run across the water's surface to gather speed.

Mute Swans (left) were introduced from Europe and are common year-round in eastern park lakes. Weighing up to 30 pounds and with a 6-foot wingspan, they are identified by their graceful curved necks, orange and black bills and raised wings. **Trumpeter Swans** (below) are the rarest of the three. Thousands of swan skins were collected for the millinery trade in the late 1800s, severely threatening the swan population. The birds have made a comeback from near extinction, and now their loud bugling can be heard again in secluded lakes in the Pacific Northwest.

The 11 subspecies of **Canada Geese** *(left)* vary in size from 3 to 30 pounds. All look alike with the typical white chin straps. The smallest and rarest subspecies breeds in the Aleutian Islands of Alaska. Foxes introduced by fur farmers ravaged the population until only one breeding island remained. However, Aleutian Canada Geese have begun to return to other islands that have been cleared of foxes, and the small flock migrates across the Pacific Ocean to the Central Valley of California. Canada Geese migration patterns have been affected by modern technology. When mechanical corn pickers leaves grain in the fields, some subspecies abbreviate or forego migration all together because their needs can be met where they breed. Geese are becoming increasingly common in reserves where hunting is prohibited. Like swans, geese mate for life and both parents vigorously protect the **goslings** *(right)* until they can fly south with the parents.

Snow Geese *(above),* the most abundant goose species, breeds in the Alaskan and Canadian Arctic and vast numbers winter along the American coastline. These large snow-white geese have black wingtips, a feature shared with other white birds like Wood Storks, White Ibises, White Pelicans and Whooping Cranes. The black wingtips make white wings appear more conspicuous and may prevent midair collisions.

The diminutive **Ross' Geese** are virtually identical to Snow Geese except for body size. They are the smallest North American goose and the entire population numbers only 15,000. This species winters in the agricultural valleys of Central California. Brant are small, dark, sea geese. Exclusively marine in winter, they feed on eelgrass and algae on tidal flats along both coasts. From the great eelgrass pastures of the Aleutian Islands, Brant Geese migrate to the lagoons of Mexico, a flight that can take them as little as three days!

Ducks

The mating behavior of ducks is the opposite of that of geese and swans; ducks mate with different partners each season. Males initially set up and defend territories but abandon them after mating. They then begin a flightless stage when they molt their breeding feathers and assume their 'eclipse' plumage, resembling females. When fully refeathered, they join other males and migrate south. Females protect against marsh predators like raccoons and snapping turtles. While the young are flightless, the females molt. When refeathered, the family migrates south.

Pintails *(above)* are handsome ducks that form large wintering flocks together with Mallards and American Wigeons. Wigeons utter a peculiar whistling quack while they feed. Shovelers are patterned like Mallards except for their unique spatulate bill, with which they sieve animal and plant foods from lake bottoms and pond surfaces. Blue-winged and Green-winged teals are the smallest ducks, yet they can fly as fast as 160 miles an hour and migrate about 125 miles per day.

Wood Ducks *(left)* live in trees as high as 60 feet off the ground. Conservationists aid this attractive duck by placing nest boxes in wooded swamps. The female incubates the eggs until they hatch and calls to her downy young, who step into the air and flutter helplessly to the water. Soon they learn to fly with great skill through a maze of trees.

Dabbling, or surface feeding, ducks are generally found in freshwater environments and eat seeds and vegetation found along pond margins. **Mallards** *(below)* are the most common duck in North America. The male's metallic green head is familiar to anyone who has ever visited a duckpond.

Mallard's interbreed with these related species as well as domesticated European ducks to produce hybrids. The **American Widgeon** *(right)* or Baldpate, breeds from California to the Arctic, and likes wild celery. The **Blue-winged Teal** *(above)* migrates to South America.

Grebes, like loons, are adapted to diving, but while loons are fisheaters, grebes will take aquatic insects as well. Because their legs are placed so far back, grebes walk with difficulty on land but with ease on water. The mating dance of the **Western Grebe** *(right)* is a water ballet. Both partners rise up and skitter across the lake on webbed feet. **Horned Grebes** *(left)* and **Eared Grebes** *(above)* are so named for their ornamental breeding plumes. Pied-billed Grebes are duck-like birds with chicken-like beaks and rarely fly. They are freshwater inhabitants that can slowly sink until completely submerged.

Anhingas are another submarine diving species. In slow-moving streams of the South, Anhingas, or Snakebirds, spear prey underwater. When a fish is secured, Anhingas will surface and swallow it head first to avoid the spines. Related to cormorants, Anhingas also lack waterproofing. To avoid becoming waterlogged, they must 'hang' their wings half open to dry.

GAMEBIRDS

Gamebirds of North America include such groups as waterfowl, chicken-like birds, and doves and pigeons. The first is covered under different headings. Gallinaceous, or chicken-like, birds are hunted for sport and meat throughout major upland habitats of North America. Many state game departments have active programs to enhance populations through releases, habitat maintenance, food and cover planting, and bag limits.

Most birds in this group are nonmigratory vegetarians favoring high-fiber diets of tender buds, grains, berries and nuts. All are ground nesters, and their eggs are cyptically colored and laid in a nest hidden in dense cover. The female incubates for 3 to 4 weeks and is solely responsible for raising the chicks. At hatching, downy chicks are able to elude danger by running for cover. Raccoons, opossums, skunks, hawks and foxes are natural predators. Eating insects and vegetable foods, the chicks grow quickly and fledge. Females can nest twice in a good season.

In general, grouse are naturally tame, but their behavior becomes wary with hunting experience. 'Fool hens' are the vernacular name for **Spruce Grouse** *(below)* and **Blue Grouse** of northern coniferous forests. They eat spruce buds and needles, insects and mushrooms. Black-bellied males spread out a white collar of feathers to expose their red air sacs in a display similar to the Ruffed Grouse. Females, dappled in brown plumage, are inconspicuous as they sit on mossy nests.

Montezuma, or **Harlequin Quail** *(left)* is a Mexican species that is found in the mountains of the extreme Southwest. The male's harlequin facial pattern is unique among gamebirds. Like most quail, these birds frequent special areas for dust baths each day.

Doves and pigeons are small-head and short-legged birds that are typically swift in flight. Doves are generally ground-feeding gamebirds that select seeds, grain and fallen fruit, buds, young grasses and insects. **White-winged Doves** *(left)* are locally abundant in the brushlands of the Southwest. Large flocks of this species arrive from Mexico in the early spring to nest in mesquite scrub. **Mourning Doves** *(above)* nest throughout North America and are named for their cooing call. Their swift, direct flight provides an ample challenge for the huntsman. They are the most hunted gamebird in North America, with over 30 million bagged each year. In California alone almost 3 million are taken. Doves are dependent on farmlands for food and nest in brushy trees. The parents feed the young a milky substance produced from the foods they eat.

Gambel's Quail *(above)* and California Quail are common western game-birds found around dense brushy habitats. California Quail prefer desert areas while the similar Gambel's Quail can tolerate residential lands and damp areas quite well. Both have distinctive topknots that look like floating apostrophes. Scaled and **Mountain Quail** *(opposite)*, which occur in western mountains, also have topknots.

Rock Doves, or Domestic Pigeons are common city dwellers of the world. They, along with homing pigeons and fancy pigeons, derive from cliff-nesting birds of Europe and Asia. White-crowned Pigeons breed in the mangrove swamps of the Florida Keys. **Band-tailed Pigeons** *(left)* are common in evergreen and deciduous forests of the Pacific Northwest, and Red-billed Pigeons occur in south Texas where mature trees occur near agriculture lands. Ground Doves are a small, short-tailed species common in weedy, southern bottomlands. These doves act like quail by remaining still until almost stepped on, at which point they zig-zag off into the undergrowth.

SEABIRDS

The cry of a gull on a lonely beach captures the essence of the sea. Soaring overhead on brisk winds or buoyantly floating amid crashing waves, gulls share the ocean with over 70 species of seabirds. These include bird families known to beachcombers and sailors alike: albatross, shearwaters and storm-petrels; cormorants, pelicans, gannets and boobies; gulls, terns and jaegers; and puffins and auks.

Seabirds are well adapted to the marine environment. Webbed feet serve as more than paddles for some. Pelagic Cormorant's control egg temperatures with their feet. Tufted Puffins dig burrows in rocky soil with theirs. Petrels 'walk on water' like their namesake Saint Peter while looking for food. Pigeon Guillemots display their bright red feet during courtship displays.

Seabirds also have multi-purpose beaks. Puffins, with crescent-shaped bills, can catch and carry many small minnows at once without dropping them. During mating season, the males attract females with their brightly colored, masklike beaks. White Pelicans scoop up large fish with their expandable bill pouch, and in hot weather, pelicans stay cool by fluttering loose throat skin. Western Gulls grab food off the water's surface with their stout bills. Their yellow bills have a dot of red near the tip that chicks instinctively peck, stimulating the parents to disgorge a predigested meal.

Each seabird has a specific manner of fishing. Cormorants propell themselves with their powerful legs while Common Murres literally fly underwater with their wings. Plunging from heights over 60 feet, Brown Pelicans and Caspian Terns are spectacular divers. Sooty Shearwaters seize minute crustacea from the sea's surface. Black Skimmers rip along the water's surface with their lower bill tip submersed. Upon contact with surface-feeding fish, the knife-like upper bill snaps shut instantly.

Albatross, shearwaters and storm petrels have special 'tubenoses' to help them survive in the marine environment. Glands in these external tubular nostrils concentrate salt, which is then excreted in drops. Laysan and Black-footed Albatross occur in deep waters off the continental shelf and breed in the remote northwestern Hawaiian Islands. The albatross wing is a forerunner of the airplane wing: a hollow bone reinforced with internal struts. With their unusually long wingspread, albatrosses are masters of flight, and during storms they glide and bank in gale force winds because it is safer to be airborne than on the water!

Puffins, like penguins, can swim underwater with their flipperlike wings, but unlike penguins, they can also fly even though their short wings make it difficult for them to get airborne. This is one reason they nest on high cliffs. To gain momentum for flight, **Horned Puffins** *(left)* jump off the cliff's edge.

Long considered a symbol of good luck, as mariners throughout the world often encountered them in fair weather, or when the weather was soon to change for the better, the wide-winged **Albatross** *(below)* is a canny glider. Its name comes from Arabic for 'bucket'. Originally intended for the pelican's beak, the tag came to rest on simply the largest seagoing bird spotted by sailors, and it stuck.

With a bill almost half as long as its body, **Brown Pelicans** *(below)* appear clumsy on land but fly with ease and dive expertly *(right)*. Brown Pelicans are making a comback after suffering from pesticides, which affected their egg-laying ability. **White Pelicans** *(above)* frequent large western lakes, where flocks of them herd fish into shallow water and scoop them up. In the breeding season, White Pelicans develop horny growths atop their bills, but their function remains unknown.

Gannets *(left)* colonize in northeastern Canada and Maine. These white birds dive head first from great heights to catch schooling fish. Gannets are closely related to boobies of the tropical seas.

Ring-billed and **California Gulls** *(above)* nest on inland lakes and help farmers by eating insects—a fact which Mormons commemorate. In 1848 the struggling Mormon colony in Salt Lake City, Utah faced starvation because long-horned grasshoppers (Mormon crickets) consumed their crops. Large flocks of California Gulls descended on the plague, devoured the grasshoppers and saved the Mormons. Their prayers answered, Mormons built a monument to the gulls.

Caspian Terns *(right)*, the largest terns in North America, weigh just over one pound and have dagger-sharp blood-red bills. **Least Terns** are the smallest, weighing two ounces, and they have delicate yellow bills. **Arctic Terns** are capable of sustained flight by continually flapping their wings. Commuting over 22,000 miles between polar regions, they spend more time in constant sunlight than any other creature.